Published in 2013 by The Rosen Publishing Group, Inc.
29 East 21st Street, New York, NY 10010

Photo Credits: **KEY** tl=top left; tc=top center; tr=top right; cl=center left; cr=center right; bl=bottom left; bc=bottom center; br=bottom right; bg=background
CBT = Corbis; DT = Dreamstime; iS = istockphoto.com; SH = Shutterstock; TF = Topfoto; TPL = photolibrary.com; wiki = Wikipedia
front cover SH; **4–5**cl SH; **6–7**cr CBT; **8**br, tl CBT; **8–9**bg SH; **9**br, cl, tr CBT; **10**cr CBT; bc iS; **10–11**bg SH; **11**br, cl CBT; tr TF; **12**bc SH; tr TPL; **13**bc, cr CBT; **14**bc CBT; bl iS; bc, br SH; **14–15**bg iS; **15**bc, tl, tr CBT; **16**bc CBT; bc, bl, br iS; **17**bc, bc, bl, br iS; **18**br iS; bc, bl wiki; **18–19**bg iS; **19**bc, bl CBT; br iS; bc wiki; **20**tc CBT; br TPL; **21**tc TF; bc TPL; **24**bl DT; cr, tl, tr SH; **24–25**bg SH; **25**bc SH; **26**bc, tr CBT; **27**bc CBT; tr iS; **28**bl, tc SH; **29**tc iS; **30**cr SH

All illustrations copyright Weldon Owen Pty Ltd

Weldon Owen Pty Ltd
Managing Director: Kay Scarlett
Creative Director: Sue Burk
Publisher: Helen Bateman
Senior Vice President, International Sales: Stuart Laurence
Vice President Sales North America: Ellen Towell
Administration Manager, International Sales: Kristine Ravn

Library of Congress Cataloging-in-Publication Data

Steele, Kathryn.
 Stones and bones : archaeology in action / by Kathryn Steele.
     p. cm. — (Discovery education: ancient civilizations)
 Includes index.
 ISBN 978-1-4777-0053-2 (library binding) — ISBN 978-1-4777-0091-4 (pbk.) —
 ISBN 978-1-4777-0092-1 (6-pack)
 1. Antiquities—Juvenile literature. 2. Archaeology—Juvenile literature. I. Title.
 CC171.S73 2013
 930.1—dc23
                                 2012019808

Manufactured in the United States of America

CPSIA Compliance Information: Batch #W13PK2: For Further Information contact Rosen Publishing, New York, New York at 1-800-237-9932

ANCIENT CIVILIZATIONS

STONES AND BONES
ARCHAEOLOGY IN ACTION

KATHRYN STEELE

PowerKiDS
press

New York

Contents

The Buried Past

People leave traces of their lives behind. Items they use are dropped or discarded. Buildings are abandoned or destroyed. Bodies are buried in graves and tombs. In time, soil covers this material. Then the process is repeated. In this way, archaeological sites build up over time. They can be many feet (m) thick and go back thousands of years. Processes of decay destroy much of what is buried. Even so, some evidence is preserved, waiting to be rediscovered. Archaeologists carefully excavate sites that they locate, then analyze what they have found. They learn about the people who once lived there—their food, clothes, and homes, and the lives they led.

Tools
Simple trowels and brushes are the tools archaeologists use the most, since they can excavate delicate objects with them. New technology has expanded the range of equipment used today.

Dig at the Louvre

Before new sections of the Louvre art gallery in Paris, France, were built, a team of archaeologists excavated the site. They found thousands of objects going back 700 years.

Digging at the Site

I n the early days of archaeology, digging was often disorganized or careless. When Heinrich Schliemann searched for the ancient city of Troy in the 1870s, he dug right through the site until he reached fortifications in the lower levels. Crucial evidence from the upper layers was lost or destroyed. Scientific digging methods have developed since then. Careful planning occurs before a dig. Samples of soil and other material are taken for analysis. During excavations, finds, larger features, and relationships between features are mapped and recorded.

1. Grid planning
Archaeologists establish a grid plan before any digging starts. They give each square on the plan a reference number.

2. Marking out the area
Usually only some site areas are chosen for excavation and marked out with pegs and string according to the plan.

3. Excavation

The team digs inside marked areas. They pay attention to changes in the layers to learn how the site was formed.

4. Finding artifacts

When artifacts are found, the location is recorded and photos are taken. Finds may be removed from the site.

5. Keeping records

As archaeologists excavate, they take notes on finds, soil, and other details. These notes are referred to later on.

In the Laboratory

Finds and samples are taken to the laboratory, where different specialists can examine them to gather more information. For example, all the pottery pieces from a particular site are sorted and compared. Archaeologists study the different types of pots to determine their uses and their origins. There may be many imported jugs, for example, which would show trade connections. Examining a shard under a microscope may reveal the clay that was used to make it and where that clay came from. Chemically analyzing residue in a pot may reveal what it once held.

1. Unpacking
After being transported from the site to the laboratory, which is often in a museum or university, finds are carefully unpacked.

2. Sorting
Artifacts are sorted, often into the type of artifact or the site layer that it came from. This is a preliminary step in analysis.

3. Cleaning
When artifacts come out of the ground, they need to be cleaned before they can be examined or even recognized.

4. Cataloging
All artifacts are labeled with an identifying number. Details about the object are recorded beside this number in a catalog system.

5. Analyzing
Artifacts are analyzed to learn more about them. Here, two archaeologists study a wallet from the Civil War era.

Early Humans

Archaeologists have learned much about our ancient ancestors. In southeastern Africa between 2 and 3 million years ago, the hominid branch of primates thrived on grassy plains. They walked on two feet, which left their hands free to carry things and make stone tools. About 2.3 million years ago, new species of the genus *Homo* emerged. Large brains made them intelligent and adaptable. It is thought that modern humans, *Homo sapiens sapiens,* evolved in Africa between 200,000 and 100,000 years ago and spread from there.

Lucy's bones
Archaeologists found about 40 percent of an early hominid's fossilized skeleton in Ethiopia. They called the hominid Lucy.

First australopithecines
4.2 million BC
Apelike creatures who walked upright first appeared in Africa. Some were probably ancestors of modern humans.

Hand axes
1.6 million BC
Large, symmetrical hand axes marked an advance in stone tool technology. Later forms of *Homo* moved farther into Europe.

First use of fire
458,000 BC
At Zhoukoudian, China, burned animal bones found with stone tools suggested hominids were using fire in a controlled way.

First carvings
35,000 BC
Modern humans living in Europe were associated with burial sites and art objects such as bone and ivory carvings of animals.

MARY LEAKEY

At Laetoli in Tanzania in 1978, Mary Leakey and her team began excavating two sets of hominid footprints that were created about 3.6 million years ago. At that time, an adult and child had walked through recently fallen volcanic ash, which hardened. Soon afterward, more ash fell and sealed the footprints. This is the earliest direct evidence of human bipedalism, that is, walking upright on two feet.

Mary Leakey with casts of two Laetoli hominid footprints

Tool maker

Around 2.5 million years ago in Africa, early *Homo* species began to use pebbles from riverbeds to make rough chopping tools.

**Female statuettes
26,000 BC**

Carved female figurines were found from France to Russia. This suggested widespread contact between different groups across Europe.

**First fired clay pottery
14,000 BC**

The Jōmon people of Honshu, Japan, made the first pottery to be baked in fire. The pots were used for eating and to store food.

**First domestic animal
10,000 BC**

In Germany and the eastern Mediterranean, humans had domesticated dogs. Wolves may have been trained for hunting much earlier.

**Sumerian writing
5200 BC**

The first writing system developed. It was called cuneiform. Marks were made in wet clay with wedge-shaped tools.

Early Cities

The development of agriculture meant people produced more food than they could eat in one season. The surplus was stored and traded. While some people farmed, others specialized in skills such as making pottery, weaving, building, trading, and even fighting. Administration and ruling became a speciality because as settlements got bigger, they needed organization to keep them running smoothly. The biggest settlements were cities, with monumental buildings, fortifications, and networks of roads, which could be built using the large workforce that was available.

Çatal Hüyük
In Turkey in about 6000 BC, an extremely large village existed. The tightly packed buildings were entered through the roof.

Egypt
From about 3500 BC
Agricultural settlements expanded along the Nile River. By 3100 BC, they had become a unified kingdom ruled by a pharaoh.

Ur
From about 3000 BC
This walled city, in what is now Iraq, had temples and palaces, and it relied on irrigation systems and trade networks.

Knossos
From about 2500 BC
This city was ruled from a palace that controlled the manufacture and trade of perfumes, ceramics, and textiles in Minoan Crete.

Babylon
From about 1700 BC
Supported by agriculture on the fertile floodplain of Iraq's Euphrates River, this walled city became the center of an empire.

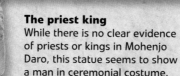

The priest king
While there is no clear evidence of priests or kings in Mohenjo Daro, this statue seems to show a man in ceremonial costume.

Mohenjo Daro
This highly organized city of the Indus Valley civilization thrived between c. 2600 and 1900 BC. Mud brick buildings were arranged in a grid.

Mayan settlements
From about 1500 BC
These Central American cities had temples and road systems. They relied on corn and other domesticated plants and animals for food.

Sparta
From about 700 BC
The citizens of this Greek city-state concentrated on building and training armies, but they also built theaters and temples.

Rome
From about 500 BC
The city grew from an agricultural settlement to be the center of the Roman Empire. Political life was focused around the forum.

Cuzco
From about AD 1300
This South American capital of the Inca was walled, with stone temples, roads, and aqueducts. It was conquered by Spanish invaders in 1533.

Temples and Pyramids

For thousands of years, people have built places to worship their gods. Rulers also built them to impress their people, such as the vast pyramids built by the ancient kings of Egypt. Some temples were like houses, where statues of the gods were kept, along with treasures dedicated to them. People could also visit to learn religious teachings through paintings and sculpture. Archaeologists investigate how temples were built and learn about religions and rituals. They also help conserve these buildings.

Giza, Egypt
The three pyramids at Giza were tombs for pharaohs, who were considered gods. The pyramids were part of a larger religious complex.

Horyu-ji
These Buddhist temples in Nara, Japan, were built in about AD 700. They are the world's oldest surviving wooden buildings.

The Step Pyramid, Egypt About 2750 BC
This was built as part of a ceremonial complex for Pharaoh Djoser. His followers believed he could climb the giant steps to the heavens.

The Temple Complex of Karnak, Egypt About 1550 BC
The complex included several temples, including one devoted to Amen, the Egyptian god of the empire.

Ziggurat of Ur, Iraq About 1323 BC
This temple was built to the Moon god Nanna. It was partly reconstructed in the twentieth century.

Parthenon, Greece About 448 BC
The Parthenon in Athens, Greece, was built to honor the goddess Athena. It was decorated with sculptures painted in bright colors.

That's Amazing!

Early Japanese governments sometimes moved the capital. When they did, they ordered that the most important temples be taken apart and rebuilt at the new location.

Temple of Kukulkan, Mexico
About AD 600
The largest building in the Mayan city of Chichén Itzá was a step pyramid to the snake deity, Kukulkan.

Ananda Temple, Myanmar
About AD 1105
Still maintained and in use today, this Buddhist place of worship was built in the city of Pagan by King Kyanzittha.

Angkor Wat, Cambodia
About AD 1150
This vast Hindu temple was built by the Khmer ruler Suryavarman II as part of his capital. It is dedicated to Vishnu.

Ranakpur, India
About AD 1438
This Jain temple is one of several in an isolated valley of Rajasthan, in western India. It has 24 pillared halls and 80 domes.

Tombs and Graves

Humans began to regularly bury their dead more than 30,000 years ago. Often, burials were simple—the body was interred in a grave along with a few possessions. But as societies became more complex and some people grew powerful, their tombs became more elaborate, with adornments made of gemstones and metals, as well as fine ceramic, stone, or metal vessels. Some tombs held more than one body and were used over many generations.

Lower passageway

Burial chamber
The pharaoh's preserved body was found in a sarcophagus.

Antechamber
This entryway was decorated with paintings of Seti I and Egyptian gods.

Egyptian tomb
Seti I's tomb is the longest and deepest rock-cut tomb in the Valley of the Kings. It was robbed in ancient times.

Unfinished stairway leads to bedrock.

Knowth, Ireland About 3500 BC
This passage tomb has two underground passages with carved stonework. It is covered by a mound 312 feet (95 m) across.

Kistvaen, England About 2300 BC
This type of grave was made of slabs of granite capped with a large stone, which was then covered by an earth mound.

Tholos tomb, Greece About 1500 BC
The Mycenaean tholos, or beehive, tomb was a stone chamber covered by soil. It was entered through a short passageway.

Terra-cotta warriors, China. About 210 BC
Thousands of terra-cotta warriors were buried in pits to guard the tomb of Emperor Qin Shi Huangdi.

Ready for the afterlife

Seti I ruled Egypt from 1290 to 1279 BC. His burial chamber was filled with food, possessions, and objects that he might use in the afterlife.

Catacombs, Italy
About AD 100
Jews and early Christians in Italy could not buy burial plots. They put the bodies of their dead in niches in underground tunnels.

Sipán, Peru
About AD 290
Several richly dressed leading members of the Moche people were buried with attendants under mud-brick pyramids.

Sutton Hoo, England
About AD 600
A burial in a 90-foot- (27 m) long ship's hull contained weapons and other objects made of precious metals.

Taj Mahal, India
About AD 1630
The Mogul emperor of India, Shah Jahan, had this tomb built for his wife. Made of white marble, it took 22 years to complete.

Iceman
This body found in the Italian Alps is from about 3300 BC. The man had smoke-blackened lungs from sitting by open fires.

Buried Bodies

When archaeologists find the physical remains of people from long ago, usually only the bones are left after centuries in the ground. Archaeologists who specialize in analyzing bones can often tell whether the people were male or female, how old they were, and even what injuries or illnesses they had. Sometimes, in extremely dry, wet, or cold burial conditions, the skin, hair, organs, and even stomach contents are preserved. Clothes and wooden implements can also survive. These preserved bodies are like time capsules that give us the opportunity to learn much more about how people lived.

Neu Versen Man
This red-haired man had a broken clavicle. He died between AD 220 and 430 and was found in a bog in Germany.

Lindow Man
This man was 25 years old when he was killed and thrown into a bog in England in about AD 100. His body turned black from the acidic water.

Tollund Man
Tollund Man was found in a bog in Denmark. His body dates to about 300 BC. He had been strangled, and his last meal had been gruel made of barley.

Underwater Archaeology

Many archaeological sites are found under water. For thousands of years, ships and boats have sunk in lakes, rivers, and oceans. Harbors and coastal settlements have become submerged. Some water environments preserve organic materials better than land conditions do, at least until the materials are exposed to air. For this reason, underwater sites can have wooden, cloth, and plant materials that normally would not survive. As scuba diving equipment has improved, especially with the Aqua-Lung in the 1950s, archaeologists have gained access to these unique sites.

DISINTEGRATION

Sunken ships undergo a process of decay and burial over time. Wave action and currents batter the ship, while waterborne sediments build up in and around it. Early on, the more fragile structures, such as the mast and rigging, break up. Then the upper decks suffer from wave action. The heavier structures eventually weaken and disintegrate, and sediments bury the remaining parts of the ship.

Did You Know?

Many nations do not have laws that protect shipwrecks. This means treasure hunters freely plunder these sites, something they could not do at archaeological sites on land.

Lifting equipment
Artifacts are placed on trays and floated to the surface using balloon-like bags filled with air.

Wet excavations

Underwater archaeology is a relatively new field. The digging techniques used on land have been adapted to suit the uniquely difficult conditions. Advances are being made all the time.

...ecked wooden ship

After 10 years

After 50 years

After 80 years

Diving equipment
Scuba equipment allows archaeologists to dive to sites and work for about an hour at a time.

Excavation grid
A site grid is attached to the seafloor. This helps archaeologists record the exact location of finds.

Underwater photography
Using underwater cameras, archaeologists take photos to record details of the excavation.

Vacuum cleaner
Instead of digging with a trowel, archaeologists use air-lifting pipes to suck sediment away from finds.

NAZCA LINES

LEGEND: It has been suggested that these lines and figures, made by clearing away dark rocks in the desert in southern Peru, were extraterrestrials' landing strips.

TRUTH: The Nazca people worked for centuries to create them. Similar shapes are painted on local ceramics. Wooden survey pegs were used to lay out the lines.

EASTER ISLAND

LEGEND: Comparing stone monuments in Peru and Easter Island, Norwegian anthropologist Thor Heyerdahl proposed that it was the Inca people who settled the island.

TRUTH: Comparison of languages and cultural features, along with DNA analysis of bones, confirms Easter Islanders are Polynesians.

STONEHENGE

LEGEND: Located in Southern England, these large stones were thought to be ruins of a temple built by pre-Roman druids, where they carried out rituals, including sacrifice.

TRUTH: Excavation revealed several stages of building. The last was in about 2000 BC, well before the druids.

MOUND BUILDERS

LEGEND: Vikings or Central American tribes were the ones who built the burial and ceremonial earthworks in the North American Midwest.

TRUTH: Excavation showed that the sites date from 1000 BC to AD 500, and that the mounds were built by locals.

Truth and Legend

Monuments and objects made long ago can seem strange and mysterious, and stories about the past can become distorted. Many theories have been proposed to explain why people of the past might have done something we can see no reason for. These range from the odd—Vikings built mounds in the American Midwest—to the outrageous—Stonehenge was made using magic. Archaeological investigation can add to our knowledge and also clear up controversies and lay myths to rest.

UNDERWATER CITY

LEGEND: Atlantis was an advanced culture that perished when an island blew up and sank beneath the ocean.

TRUTH: In about 1550 BC, the volcanic Greek island of Santorini erupted. Excavation of Akrotiri, a site on the island, revealed a city buried in ash.

Who Owns the Past?

Attitudes toward the past and our cultural heritage have changed greatly since the early days of archaeology. Back then, objects were often removed from countries or sold to collectors. This has caused controversy. For example, the Greek government still hopes that statues taken from the Parthenon more than 200 years ago will soon be returned to Greece. But, at present, they are still held by the British Museum in London. Today, many countries have laws to protect their archaeological heritage. However, sites are still looted and artifacts are sold illegally on the black market.

Temple of Dendur in original site
This sandstone temple was built by the Roman emperor Augustus in Egypt in about 15 BC to honor local gods.

Temple of Dendur in museum
In 1965, the Egyptian government gave the temple to the United States for helping to relocate ancient Egyptian monuments.

Parthenon sculptures in original site
After 2,000 years, few statues remain on the Parthenon in Athens, Greece. Some are on display in the Acropolis Museum, in Athens, which opened in 2007.

Parthenon sculptures in museum
Many of the Parthenon statues taken by Lord Elgin in 1801 are on display at the British Museum in London. They are also known as the Elgin Marbles.

Great Sites

n the past 250 years, archaeologists have investigated sites containing everything from scattered stone tools and isolated hominid fossils to vast temples, tombs, and city complexes. Small sites can be just as important as large ones in explaining the human past. But it is the larger sites that attract most attention, with millions of tourists journeying to see them each year. Investigations continue at many of these sites. Archaeologists add more detail to what they already know and develop new interpretations to explain new discoveries.

Petra, Jordan
Hidden in a desert canyon, this site is famed for its rock-cut tombs, built by the Nabataeans from about 100 BC.

NORTH AMERICA

1
2
3

SOUTH AMERICA

4

Machu Picchu, Peru
This Inca city high in the Andes has terraced fields, tombs, houses, and a temple for observing the Sun.

Colosseum, Rome
Completed in AD 80, this amphitheater was used for staging gladiatorial fights, mock sea battles, and other entertainment.

The great sites
Some of these sites are thousands of years old. They are windows into the way people once lived.

1. Mesa Verde
2. Teotihuacán
3. Chichén Itzá
4. Machu Picchu
5. Stonehenge
6. Lascaux
7. Pompeii
8. Parthenon
9. Colosseum
10. Hadrian's Wall
11. Karnak
12. Giza pyramids
13. Petra
14. Terra-cotta warriors
15. Great Wall of China
16. Angkor Wat

EUROPE

ASIA

AFRICA

AUSTRALIA

Great Wall of China
Sections of the wall were constructed between 221 BC and AD 1644 to protect the Chinese empire from invaders.

Hadrian's Wall, UK
Much of this defensive wall still stands. It was built by the Romans from AD 122 and included several forts.

What Do You Remember?

Try this quiz to see how much you can remember about what you have read.

 1 What is the name given to the female australopithecine who lived about 3.18 million years ago in Ethiopia?

 2 Where did Mary Leakey and her team find two sets of hominid footprints?

 3 What is the name of the temple that was built to honor the goddess Athena in 448 BC?

 4 What is the name given to the body from around 300 BC that was found in a bog in Denmark?

 5 Whose tomb, built around 210 BC, was filled with life-sized statues of warriors?

 6 What temple in Cambodia was built in AD 1150 and dedicated to the god Vishnu?

Answers: 1. Lucy **2.** Laetoli, Tanzania **3.** The Parthenon **4.** Tollund Man **5.** Emperor Qin Shi Huangdi **6.** Angkor Wat

Glossary

adornments
(uh-DORN-mentz) Objects used
to decorate or make attractive.

australopithecine
(aw-stray-loh-PIH-thih-zyn)
An apelike creature who walked
upright and lived in Africa more
than 3 million years ago.

controversies
(kon-truh-ver-seez)
Differences of opinion or
disputes over issues.

crucial (KROO-shul) Vital or
having a very important effect.

dedicated
(DEH-dih-kayt-ed) Set aside for
a particular purpose.

discarded (dis-KARD-ed)
Thrown away.

distorted (dih-STAWRT-ed)
Changed from the truth
or reality.

excavate (EK-skuh-vayt)
To dig up or uncover by digging,
especially in a methodical way.

forum (FOR-um) An open
public space in ancient Rome
where people could meet.

heritage (HER-uh-tij)
Something passed on from
earlier generations of a country,
family, or area.

hominid (HAH-mih-nid)
Any of a family of upright
walking primates, including
human beings.

implements
(IHM-pluh-mentz) Tools or other
devices used to carry out a task.

interpretations
(in-ter-prih-TAY-shunz)
Explanations of something or the
reasons behind it.

interred (in-TERD) Placed in
a grave or tomb.

preliminary
(prih-LIH-muh-nehr-ee)
First; before the main activity.

primates (PRY-maytz)
A group of mammals with large
brains, forward-looking eyes,
and fingers that can grasp
things. Primates include humans,
apes, and monkeys.

process (PRAH-ses) A number
of actions that, step by step,
bring about a result.

residue (REH-zih-doo)
The part of something that is left
over when most of it has gone.

shard (SHARD)
A fragment of a broken pot
made of baked clay.

speciality (SPEH-shul-tee)
An area of work or a skill that
a person concentrates on
carrying out.

species (SPEE-sheez) A group
of animals or plants that have
many characteristics in common.
Members of the same species
can mate and have offspring.

submerged (sub-MERJD)
Covered with or put under water.

surplus (SUR-plus) An amount
greater than what is necessary.
Surplus food is what is left over
after basic needs are met.

thrived (THRYVD) Succeeded
or prospered.

waterborne (WAH-ter-bohrn)
Carried or transmitted in or
by water.

Index

A
Akrotiri 25
Ananda Temple 17
Angkor Wat 17, 29, 30
australopithecine 12, 30

B
Babylon 14

C
catacomb 19
Çatal Hüyük 14
Civil War 11
Colosseum 29
cuneiform 13
Cuzco 15

D
Dendur, Temple of 26

E
Easter Island 24
Elgin Marbles 26, 27

G
Giza pyramids 16, 29
Great Wall of China 29

H
Hadrian's Wall 29
hand axes 12
Homo sapiens sapiens 12
Horyu-ji 16, 17

J
Jōmon 13

K
Karnak 16, 29
Kistvaen 18
Knossos 14
Knowth 18
Kukulkan 17

L
Laetoli, Tanzania 13, 30
Lascaux 29
Leakey, Mary 13, 30
Louvre 7
Lucy 12, 30

M
Machu Picchu 28, 29
Mayan settlements 15

Mohenjo Daro 15
mounds 24, 25

N
Nazca lines 24
Neu Versen Man 20
Nile River 14

S
Schliemann, Heinrich 8
Seti I 18, 19
Sipán 19
Sparta 15
Stonehenge 24, 25, 29
Sutton Hoo 19

T
Taj Mahal 19
Teotihuacán 29
Terra-cotta warriors 18, 29
Tholos tomb 18
Tollund Man 21
Troy 8

Z
Zhoukoudian 12
Ziggurat 16

Websites

Due to the changing nature of Internet links, PowerKids Press has developed an online list of websites related to the subject of this book. This site is updated regularly. Please use this link to access the list: www.powerkidslinks.com/disc/archa/